颐和园

THE SUMMER PALACE
LE PALAIS D'ÉTÉ
DER SOMMERPALAST

新世界出版社
NEW WORLD PRESS

颐和园

颐和园导游略图

TOURIST GUIDE SKETCH MAP OF THE SUMMER PALACE
PLAN DU PALAIS D'ÉTÉ YIHEYUAN-REISEKARTE

Northern Palace Gate
北宫门

Ruyi Gate
如意门

苏州街
Suzhou Street

万寿山
Longevity Hill

排云殿
Cloud-Dispelling H

长 廊
Long Corridor

石舫
Marble Boat

玉带桥
Jade Belt Bridge

昆 明 湖
Kunming Lake

Pala

Knowing Sp

南湖岛
South Lake Island

西湖
Western Lake

西
Western Dike
堤

养 水 湖
Yangshui Lake

景明楼
Building of Bright Scenery

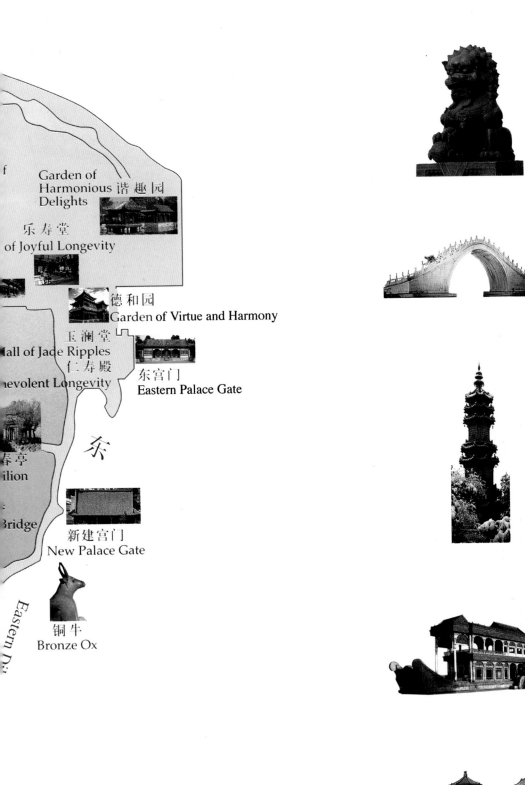

f

Garden of
Harmonious 谐趣园
Delights

乐 寿 堂
of Joyful Longevity

德和园
Garden of Virtue and Harmony

玉 澜 堂
Hall of Jade Ripples
仁 寿 殿
evolent Longevity

东宫门
Eastern Palace Gate

东

亭
ilion

Bridge

新建宫门
New Palace Gate

铜 牛
Bronze Ox

Eastern Pa...

南如意门
South Ruyi Gate

Outside the Eastern Palace Gate stands an archway carved with dragons and phoenixes. It consists of three gates, four pillars and seven towers. It is the first sight visitors see before entering the Summer Palace.

Le grand portique peint de dragons et de phénix et composé de trois portes, quatre colonnes et sept tours, est la première image que l'on voit avant d'entrer au Palais d'Eté.

Der Ehrenbogen, mit geschnitzten und bemalten Drachen- und Phönixmustern verziert, ragt außerhalb des Ostpalasttors empor. Er besteht aus drei Eingängen, vier Säulen und sieben Türmen und ist die erste Szenerie, die man vor dem Sommerpalast sieht.

The Eastern Palace Gate of the Summer
Palace, an example of the perfect combination
of palace and gardens.

La porte est du Palais d'Eté qui regroupe des
palais impériaux et des jardins.

Das Ostpalasttor, ein Bauwerk, das sich aus
kaiserlichem Palast und Parkanlage
zusammensetzt.

One of the bronze lions
guarding the gates of the
Summer Palace

Lion en bronze, gardien du
Palais d'Eté.

Ein bronzener Löwe

頤和園

Kylin, a Chinese unicorn

Qilin, licorne chinoise

Ein bronzenes Qilin
(chinesisches Fabeltier)

◄ Stone staircase carved with
dragons in front of the main
gate of the Summer Palace

Les perrons sculptés de
dragons devant la porte est.

Die Drachensteinschnitzerei
auf der Treppen vor dem
Ostpalasttor

Portrait of Emperor
Qianlong

Portrait de l'empereur
Qianlong

Das Porträt des Kaisers
Qianlong

The Summer Palace, formerly called the Garden of Pure
Ripple, is located at the foot of the western hills of Beijing,
about 15 kilometers from downtown Beijing. It was started in
1750 (in the 15th year of the reign of Qianlong of the Qing
Dynasty) by Qianlong for the 60th birthday of his mother,
Dowager Xiaosheng. It cost 140 tons of silver, took 15 years
to build, and was completed in 1764. It was burnt down
along with the Old Summer Palace in 1860 when the Anglo-
French joint forces invaded Beijing.

Le Palais d'Eté, anciennement Qingyiyuan, situé près des
collines de l'ouest de Beijing, à 15 km de la ville, fut construit
entre 1750 et 1764 par l'empereur Qianlong des Qing pour
célébrer le 60° anniversaire de sa mère, impératrice
douairière Xiaosheng, au coût de 140 tonnes d'argent. En
1860 (dixième année du règne de l'empereur Xianfeng), les
envahisseurs anglais et français le détruisirent et brûlèrent le
Yuanmingyuan.

Der Sommerpalast (Yiheyuan), ursprünglich Qingyiyuan
(Garten des Reinen Wassers) genannt, liegt am Fuß des
Westbergs bei Beijing, etwa 15 km vom Stadtgebiet entfernt.
Mit dem Bau wurde 1750 (15. Jahr der Regierungsperiode
Qianlong) begonnen. Anläßlich des 60. Geburtstags seiner
Mutter, Kaiserinwitwe Xiaosheng, ließ der Kaiser Qianlong
diesen Garten errichten. Der Bau dauerte 15 Jahre und
erforderte 140 t Silber. 1764 wurde der Garten fertiggestellt.
1860 (10. Jahr der Regierungsperiode Xianfeng) drangen die
britisch-französischen alliierten Truppen in Beijing ein und
zerstörten gleichzeitig der Brandschatzung des
Yuanmingyuan den Yiheyuan.

Portrait of Emperor
Qianlong (1736-1795)

Portrait de l'empereur
Qianlong (1736-1795)

Das Porträt des Kaisers
Qianlong (1736-1795)

Dowager Cixi at the Summer Palace

L'impératrice douairière Cixi au Palais d'Eté (photo).

Kaiserinwitwe Cixi in Yiheyuan (Foto)

Cixi meets with the wives of foreign envoys at the Summer Palace.

L'impératrice douairière Cixi reçut en audience au Palais d'Eté les épouses des ambassadeurs étrangers.

Kaiserinwitwe Cixi empfing die Madame ausländischer Gesandter in Yiheyuan.

Portrait of Dowager Cixi

Portrait de Cixi

Das Porträt der Kaiserinwitwe Cixi

In 1886 Dowager Cixi, who held the court from behind a screen, diverted money originally designated for the Chinese navy into the reconstruction of the Garden of Pure Ripple, and renamed it Yiheyuan, meaning good health and longevity.

Cixi retained political and military power during the reigns of Tongzhi and Guangxu, from a coup d'etat in 1861 until her death in 1908, 48 years in total. The Summer Palace is the place where she handled court issues and spent most of her time.

En 1886, Cixi détourna les fonds destinés à la marine pour reconstruire le Qingyiyuan et le renomma Yiheyuan (Palais d'Eté) qui signifie le «palais du repos et de l'harmonie». La reconstruction dura 10 ans.

Pendant une période de 48 ans après 1861, année où eut lieu un coup d'État, jusqu'à sa mort en 1908, Cixi exerça les pouvoirs politiques et militaires «derrière le rideau» sous le règne des empereurs Tongzhi et Guangxu. Elle résidait souvent au Yiheyuan et y traitait les affaires d'État.

1886 riß die Kaiserinwitwe Cixi die Staatsmacht an sich und ließ sofort die Marineausgaben für den Wiederaufbau des Qingyiyuan abzweigen. Die Restauration nahm etwa zehn Jahre in Anspruch, und der Garten wurde in den heutigen Namen „Yiheyuan" umbenannt, die Zusammensetzung „Yihe" bedeutet, daß man sich seines Lebensabends erfreut.

Von der Reform 1861 in Beijing bis zu ihrem Tod 1908 hatte Cixi die Staatsmacht 48 Jahre lang während der Regierungsperiode der beiden Kaiser Tongzhi und Guangxu inne. Die Sommerpalast war eine Stätte, in der sie Staatsgeschäfte erledigte und ständig wohnte.

颐和园

Longevity Hill at sunset

La Colline de la Longévité
(Wanshou Shan) au
crépuscule.

Der Berg der Langlebigkeit
(Wanshou-Berg) in der
Abenddämmerung

The Palace of Benevolent Longevity is the place where Emperor Guangxu (1875-1908) and Dowager Cixi held court and met their ministers.

C'est dans la Salle de la Bienveillance et de la Longévité (Renshou Dian) que l'impératrice douairière Cixi et l'empereur Guangxu traitaient les affaires d'État entre 1875 et 1908.

Die Halle des Wohlwollens und der Langlebigkeit (Renschoudian) war eine Halle, in der Kaiserinwitwe Cixi und Kaiser Guangxu (1875-1908) Staatsgeschäfte führten.

Kylin in front of Palace of
Benevolent Longevity. Kylin is
a legendary animal in China
and symbolizes good luck.

Licorne, animal mythique
chinois qui symbolise la paix,
devant la Salle de la
Bienveillance et de la
Longévité.

Qilin (ein chinesisches
Fabeltier, ein glückliches
Vorzeichen)

A view inside the Palace of Benevolent Longevity

Interieur de la Salle de la Bienveillance et de la Longevite.

Innenansicht von Renshoudian

颐和园

Wenchang Pavilion is on the eastern bank of Kunming Lake. The God of Wenchang, a legendary god in control of official rank, is worshipped at the city gate.

Pavillon du Dieu de la littérature (Wenchang Ge), au bord est du lac Kunming. Selon une légende populaire, cette divinité octroyait les honneurs et les titres aux hommes.

Pavillon Blühender Kultur (Wenchangge) liegt am Ostufer des Kunming-Sees. Im Turm wurde dem Wenchang-Kaiser, einem Gott, der nach der Volkssage für akademische und amtliche Würden auf der Erde zuständig sei, Opfer dargebracht.

In 1898 when the Wuxu Reform Movement supported by Emperor Guangxu, was crushed by Cixi, the grand Hall of Jade Ripples was turned into a cell to imprison Guangxu, who remained there till his death in 1908 at the age of 38.

Après l'echec du mouvement reformiste dirige en 1898 par l'empereur Guangxu, ce dernier fut sequestre par Cixi dans la Salle des Vagues de Jade pendant dix ans jusqu'à sa mort en 1908, à l'âge de 38 ans.

Die Reform 1898, die Kaiser Guangxu einleitete, wurde von der Kaiserinwitwe Cixi unterdrückt. Danach wurde die prächtige Yulantang für Kaiser Guangxu zu einer Gefangniszelle. Er wurde hier zehn Jahre eingesperrt, bis er 1908 im Alter von 38 Jahren starb.

Emperor Guangxu
L'empereur Guangxu
Kaiser Guangxu

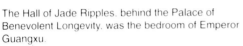

The Hall of Jade Ripples, behind the Palace of
Benevolent Longevity, was the bedroom of Emperor
Guangxu.

La Salle des Vagues de Jade (Yulan Tang), situee
derriere la Salle de la Bienveillance et de la Longevite,
ou logeait l'empereur Guangxu.

Die Halle der Jadewellen (Yulantang) hinter
Renshoudian war das Gemach des Kaisers Guangxu.

Hall of Jade Ripples

Vue extérieure de la Salle des
Vagues de Jade.

Außenansicht von Yulantang

The bedroom of Emperor Guangxu (Xinuange) remains as it was nearly a century ago.

La chambre de l'ouest (Xinuange) de la Salle des Vagues de Jade était la chambre à coucher de l'empereur Guangxu. Depuis plus de 90 ans, elle est restée inchangée.

Westgemach (Xinuange) in der Yulantang war das Gemach des Kaisers Guangxu. Obwohl über 90 Jahre verstrichen sind, bleiben die Ausstattungen nun in ihrem ursprünglichen Zustand erhalten.

Hall of Joyful Longevity, the living quarters of Dowager Cixi. In the garden Yulan magnolia, flowering crabapple and other precious flowers and plants thrive to grow tall and strong.

Vue extérieure de la Salle de la Joie et de la Longévité (Leshou Tang) où logeait l'impératrice douairière Cixi. On voit dans la cour un grand magnolia blanc, des pommiers sauvages et d'autres plantes et fleurs rares.

Außenansicht der Halle der Freude und der Langlebigkeit (Leshoutang) Leshoutang war das Gemach der Kaiserinwitwe Cixi. Im Hof wachsen wertvolle und seltene Blumen und Bäume wie gigantischer Chinesischer Lilienbaum und herbstfrüchtige Zierapfelbäume.

An interior view of the Hall of Joyful Longevity

Intérieur de la Salle de la Joie et de la Longévité.

Innenansicht von Leshoutang

The bedroom of the Dowager Cixi

Chambre à coucher de l'impératrice douairière Cixi.

Das Gemach der Kaiserinwitwe Cixi

Li Lianying (first right) and
Dowager Cixi in front of Hall of
Everlasting Longevity

Li Lianying (1er à droite) et Cixi
devant la Salle de la Joie et de
la Longévité.

Li Lianying (l. v. r.) und
Kaiserinwitwe Cixi vor
Leshoutang

Palace maid of the
Qing Dynasty

Fille d'honneur à la
Cour impériale des
Qing.

Eine Hofdame der
Qing-Dynastie

The Hall of Everlasting Longevity which was once the residence of Li Lianying, Cixi's favorite eunuch.

Pavillon de la Longévité éternelle (Yongshou Zhai), demeure de Li Lianying, eunuque de confiance de Cixi.

Das Zimmer der Ewigen Langlebigkeit (Yongshouzhai) war der Wohnort von Li Lianying, dem Obereunuchen und Favoriten der Kaiserinwitwe Cixi.

Fan Hall, at the western yard of the Hall of Joyful Longevity, is a peculiar building. It was named after Fanning the Righteous Wind. That's why every part of the hall from the ridge to the walls, windows and floor was shaped like a fan.

La cour ouest de la Salle de la Joie et de la Longévité est une construction de style particulier portant le nom de Yangrenfeng qui signifie «faire rayonner la bienveillance». Cet édifice est caractérisé par le toit, les murs, les fenêtres et le plancher en forme d'éventail.

Der Westseitenhof von Leshoutang ist ein einzigartig geformtes Bauwerk und heißt Yangrenfeng. Das bedeutet, die humanitäre und gerechte Verhaltensweise zu entwickeln. Der Name Yangrenfeng stammt aus dem Fächer. Deshalb sind das Dach, die Wände, die Fenster und der Boden fächerförmig.

The Great Stage Tower in the Garden of Virtue and Harmony has three stories and is 21 meters high and 17 meters wide. It is where the Dowager Cixi and emperors enjoyed performances 92 years ago and is one of the few intact ancient stage towers in China.

Le Théâtre impérial dans le Jardin de l'Harmonie vertueuse, à trois étages, haut de 21 m et large de 17 m, est le théâtre ancien le plus parfaitement conservé en Chine. Il était réservé, il y a une centaine d'années, à l'impératrice douairière Cixi et à l'empereur.

Die Große Theaterbühne im Garten der Tugend und Harmonie (Deheyuan), eine bisher gut erhaltende Theaterbühne aus der alten Zeit Chinas, hat drei Stockwerke und ist 21 m hoch und 17 m breit. Vor 92 Jahren sahen sich die Kaiserinwitwe Cixi und der Kaiser hier Aufführungen an.

The Hall of Health and Happiness stands in front of the Great Stage Tower. Inside it there is a gold-painted enamel throne which was Cixi's special seat when she watched performances.

La Salle des Réjouissances face à la scène du théâtre. On y trouve un trône sculpté du motif «cent oiseaux s'amusent autour du phénix», réservé à l'impératrice douairière Cixi pour assister à l'opéra.

Vor der Großen Theaterbühne wurde eine Halle der Ruhe und des Friedens (Yihedian) errichtet. In der Halle ruhte ein Thronsessel mit einem Muster „Hundert Vögel zum Phönix", der speziell der Kaiserinwitwe Cixi bei Aufführungen zur Verfügung stand.

The Great Stage Tower in the Garden of Virtue and Harmony
La grande scène du théâtre.
Die Große Theaterbühne in Deheyuan

The Great Stage Tower at night
Le Théâtre impérial au clair de lune.
Die Große Theaterbühne im Mondlicht

颐和园

The Long Corridor, 728 meters long, is divided into 273 bays and contains over 8.000 color paintings. It is known as the longest painted corridor of the world. It starts at the Moon Inviting Pavilion in the east and extends to Stone Writing Pavilion in the west and is linked with Kunming Lake and the scenic areas in front of Longevity Hill.

La Longue Galerie couverte (Chang Lang), décorée de plus de 8 000 peintures en 273 sections, part à l'est de la Porte de l'Invitation de la Lune (Yaoyue Men) jusqu'au Pavillon de la Grande Pierre (Shizhang Ting) à l'ouest, reliant les constructions principales au bord nord du lac Kunming et devant la Colline de la Longévité. Elle mesure 728 m. et est la plus longue galerie du monde.

Der Lange Wandelgang hat 273 Sektoren, die mit etwa 8000 bunten Bildern bemalt sind, verläuft über 728 m vom Osten nach Westen zwischen dem Yaoyue-Tor und dem Shizhang-Pavillon, verbindet die wichtigen Bauwerke am Kunming-See und vor dem Wanshou-Berg miteinander und gilt als die längste Galerie in der Welt.

An archway in front of
Cloud-Dispelling Gate

Le grand portique
devant la Porte des
Nuages ordonnés.

Der Ehrenbogen vor der
Wolkenzerstreuenden
Halle (Paiyundian)

Cloud-Dispelling Hall is where Dowager Cixi held ceremonies
commemorating her birthdays. Every year on the tenth day of the tenth
month of Chinese lunar calendar she was greeted by the emperor,
empress, princes, princesses and ministers' inside the hall

Le Pavillon des Nuages ordonnés sert à la célébration de l'anniversaire de
l'impératrice douairière Cixi. Lors de son anniversaire (le 10 du dixième
mois lunaire), Cixi y recevait l'empereur, l'impératrice, les princes et les
ministres qui venaient lui présenter leurs vœux.

Die Paiyundian war die Stätte, wo der Geburtstag der Kaiserinwitwe Cixi
gefeiert wurde. Anläßlich ihres Geburtstags (10. des zehnten Monats des
chinesischen Mondkalenders) gratulierten ihr hier der Kaiser, Kaiserin,
Prinzen und Minister zum Geburtstag.

Twelve rocks shaped like symbolic animals stand outside the Cloud-Dispelling Hall, and denote the year of a person's birth in China.

Les pierres des douze animaux du zodiaque chinois en dehors du Pavillon des Nuages ordonnés.

Die verschiedengestaltigen Zwölf-Tierzeichen-Steine für die zwölf Erdzweige (zur Zuordnung von Geburtsjahren im chinesischen Horoskop) außerhalb von Paiyundian

The throne in the Cloud-Dispelling Hall
Le trône de Cixi dans le Pavillon des Nuages ordonnés.
Der Thronsessel von Cixi in Paiyundian

The Revolving Scripture Repository served as
a site where imperial families kept scriptures
and statues of Buddha, and emperors and
empresses worshipped Buddha.

Le Temple des Moulins à prières ou l'on
conservait des livres bouddhiques et des
statues de Bouddha. L'empereur et
l'impératrice y allaient en pèlerinage et
récitaient les canons bouddhiques.

Zhuanglunzang war eine Stätte, wo für
Kaiserfamilie buddhistische Schriften und
Buddhastatuen aufbewahrt wurden und die
Kaiserin Sutras rezitierte.

The Pavilion of Precious Clouds. 7.55 meters high, was built of bronze and weighs 207 tons. It is a rare example of bronze architecture.

Le Pavillon des Nuages précieux (Baoyun Ge) est en bronze. Il pèse 207 tonnes et mesure 7,55 mètres, un objet très rare au monde.

Der Pavillon der Wertvollen Wolken (Baoyunge) wurde aus Bronze gegossen, wiegt 207 t und ist 7,55 m hoch. Der Bauwerk stellt eine Seltenheit seiner Art in der Welt dar.

Pavilion of Buddhist Fragrance at sunset

The Pavilion of Buddhist Fragrance is built on a huge stone foundation and is 21 meters in height. It is the place where Buddhas were enshrined by the imperial families and is also the symbol of the Summer Palace. The Pavilion of Buddhist Fragrance gives visitors a panoramic view of the Palace.

La Pagode du Parfum de Bouddha est assise sur une énorme pierre angulaire haute de 21 m. C'est un endroit où la famille impériale faisait un pèlerinage, et aussi le symbole du Palais d'Eté. De là on peut contempler tous les paysages du Palais d'Eté.

Der Pavillon des Buddhistischen Wohlgeruchs (Foxiangge) im Abendsonnenlicht Foxiangge wurde auf einem 21 m hohen Steinsockel am steilen Abhang des Wanshou-Bergs gebaut. Er war der Haustempel der Kaiserfamilie und ist auch ein Wahrzeichen des Sommerpalastes ist. Von dort aus hat man einen guten Überblick über die Landschaft des Yiheyuan.

The Bodhisattva Guanyin, enshrined inside the Pavilion of Buddhist Fragrance is 5 meters high and was made of 10 thousand catties of copper (about 6,700 kg.) in the second year of the reign of Wanli of the Ming Dynasty in 1574.

La statue d'Avalokitesvara en bronze, haute de 5 m dans la Pagode du Parfum de Bouddha (Foxiang Ge), fut fabriquée avec 5 tonnes de bronze, en 1574, autrement dit pendant la deuxième année du règne de l'empereur Wanli des Ming.

Der 5 m hohe Guanyin-Boddhisattwa in Foxiangge wurde im 2. Jahr der Regierungszeit Wanli (1574) aus Bronze gegossen.

颐和园

Pavilion of Buddhist Fragrance in spring

La Pagode du Parfum de Bouddha au printemps.

Foxiangge im Frühlingsrausch

Pavilion of Buddhist Fragrance in fall

La Pagode du Parfum de Bouddha en automne.

Foxiangge im Herbstlicht

Qingzhi Rock, also known as Rock of Dissipating a Family Fortune, is 8 meters long, 2 meters wide and 4 meters high. It was originally found in Fangshan by Mi Wanzhong, an official of the Ming Dynasty. He wanted to move it to his home and display it, but he used up all his money and had to abandon it by the roadside. When the Summer Palace was built, Emperor Qianlong ordered the rock to be brought here and named it Qingzhi Rock as it looked like a glossy ganodermá (magic fungus).

Pierre ornementale bleu vert (Qingzhixiu), appelée aussi «pierre de la famille ruinée», de 8 m de long sur 2 m de large et de 4 m de haut. Extraite à Fangshan par Mi Wanzhong, mandarin de la dynastie des Ming, elle fut pourtant abandonnée par lui en route à cause de l'épuisement de son argent. Lors de la construction du Palais d'Eté, la pierre y fut déplacée et baptisée de Qingzhixiu d'après sa couleur.

Qingzhixiu-Stein, auch Baijiashi (ein Stein, der zum Ruin einer Familie führte) genannt, ist 8 m lang, 2 m breit und 4 m hoch. Eigentlich wurde er von Mi Wanzhong, einem Beamten der Ming-Dynastie, in Fangshan abgebaut. Mi transportierte diesen Stein als Andenken nach Hause. Nachdem er aber später Bankrott gegangen war, legte er den Stein weg. Kaiser Qianlong ließ den Stein nach Yiheyuan verlagern und benannte nach dessen Farbe Qingzhixiu (grünes Schimmerndes Ganoderma-Stein).

Multi-Treasure Glazed Pagoda, which is octagonal, 16 meters high and divided into seven layers. It is covered with five-color glazed bricks and is gold plated at the top. The pagoda is built on a white Xumi stone foundations and is situated on the eastern side of Rear Hill.

La Pagode des Trésors innombrables, en briques vernissées multicolores, octogone, haute de 16 m, à sept étages, au toit doré, construite sur une terrasse de pierre blanche derrière la colline.

Die 16 m hohe Duobauliuli-Pagode (Multischatz-Glasierte-Pagode) hat sieben Werkstocke und acht Seiten, wurde mit bunten glasierten Ziegeln gemauert, die Pagodenspitze war vergoldet. Sie steht auf einem weißen Sumeru-Sockel im Osthang des Hinterbergs.

The Boundary of Popular Fragrance, is named after a place in Buddhist texts and is an archway in front of Wisdom Sea. It is built of stone and brick with five-color glazed tiles on the surface. Wisdom Sea is the highest building on Longevity Hill and its name implies that Buddha's wisdom is as boundless as the sea.

Le Portique Zhongxiangjie, arc monumental en briques vernissées, devant le Temple des Dix Mille Bouddhas (appelé aussi Mer de la Sagesse qui signifie que la sagesse de Tathagata est comme la mer sans borne), est la construction la plus haute sur la Colline de la Longévité.

Zhongxiangjie, ein buddhistischer Torbogen vor dem Zhihuihai-Tempel, war aus Ziegeln und Steinen gebaut und mit bunten glasierten Ziegeln bedeckt. Die Zhihuihai-Tempel liegt auf der höchsten Stelle des Wanshou-Bergs. „Zhihuihai" bedeutet, daß die Weisheit des Tathagata grenzenlos wie das Meer ist.

The name Four Continents is based on the Buddhist scripture which describes Xumi Mountain, the residence of Buddha, being surrounded by four continents. They are magnificent buildings with a profoundly religious atmosphere.

Le Temple des Quatre Continents (Sidabuzhou) fut construit selon les édifices autour du mont Sumeru où habitait le Bouddha. Cet ensemble d'édifices imposants a une forte couleur religieuse.

Der Tempel der Vier Großen Länder (Sidabuzhou) wurde, wie in den buddhistischen Schriften aufgezeichnet wurde, aufgrund der Vier Großen Länder um den Sumeru-Berg, wo Buddha wohnte, erbaut und ist imposant und mit religiösem Kolorit erfüllt.

A view of Four Continents
Le panorama de Sidabuzhou.
Panorama von Sidabuzhou

A snow scene at the Boundary of Popular Fragrance
Zhongxiangjie après la neige.
Zhongxiangjie im Schnee

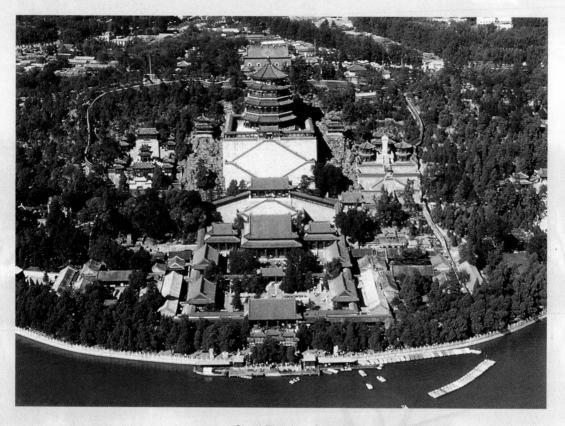

Cloud-Dispelling Gate, Second Palace Gate, Cloud-Dispelling Hall, Pavilion of Buddhist Fragrance, and Wisdom Sea in front of Longevity Hill are built on the axis line from top to bottom of the hill and from north to south. The buildings appear somber and neat.

La Porte des Nuages ordonnés, la Seconde Porte, le Pavillon des Nuages ordonnés, la Pagode du Parfum de Bouddha, la Mer de la Sagesse s'étagent de bas en haut sur l'axe sud-nord, adossés à la Colline du Parfum de Bouddha.

Die Bauten vor dem Wanshou-Berg wie das Paiyun-Tor, das Ergong-Tor, die Paiyundian, der Foxiangge und der Zhihuihai-Tempel befinden sich mit Foxiangge als Achse an beiden Seiten in Symmetrie. Von oben nach unten, von Süd nach Nord, bieten sie einen Anblick der äußerst großen Ordnung und Feierlichkeit.

A panoramic view of the main group of buildings in front of Longevity Hill taken from the top of the hill

On peut contempler au sommet de la Colline du Parfum de Bouddha les édifices principaux devant la colline.

Wenn man den Wanshou-Berg besteigt und nach Süden blickt, fallen einem alle Hauptbauten des Südhanges dieses Berges in die Augen.

Picturesque Stroll is a group of buildings including three pavilions, two towers, one corridor at the western side of Longevity Hill. Visitors walking here get the impression that they are walking through different pictures.

Le site de la Promenade dans un Tableau (Huazhongyou), situé à l'ouest de la Colline du Parfum d'Été, se compose de trois pavillons, de deux tours, d'une galerie et d'un bateau de marbre. Les paysages y sont très magnifiques.

Huazhongyou, ein Baukomplex, der aus drei Pavillons, zwei Türmen, einem Korridor und einem Torbogen besteht, liegt im Westhang des Wanshou-Bergs. Wer sich hier aufenthält, fühlt sich in einer Wunderwelt versetzt.

Pavilion of Depicting Autumn, one of the independent gardens in the Palace. It is a most attractive place in autumn.

Le Kiosque de l'Automne (Xieqiu Xuan) est l'un des édifices avec une cour. Le paysage automnal d'ici est très charmant.

Xieqiuxuan, ein Hof im Sommerpalast Im Spätherbst herrscht hier eine wunderschöne Herbststimmung und bietet sich eine faszinierende Landschaft.

Long Corridor is decorated with color paintings of figures, mountains and water, and flowers and birds on the roof and on its beams. All the paintings are exquisite and true to life. Most of them are executed within a semi-circular painted frame.

Les charpentes de la Longue Galerie couverte sont décorées de peintures représentant des personnages, des paysages de montagnes et de lacs, des fleurs et des oiseaux. Ces peintures sont vivantes, à traits précis.

Farbige Malereien am Langen Wandelgang Die Hauptmotive der farbigen Malereien sind Menschenfiguren, Landschaften, Blumen und Vögel, Felsen sowie historische und legendäre Episoden. Diese Malereien sind durch feine Führung, lebendige Ausdruck und gute Perspektive gekennzeichnet.

The zigzag Long Corridor which connects all the scenic spots on the front hill.

La Longue Galerie couverte en zigzag.

Der zickzackförmige Lange Wandelgang führt zu allen Sehenswürdigkeiten auf dem Wanshou-Berg.

Taihu Rocks at Shizhang Pavilion.

La pierre de Taihu tout près du Pavillon Shizhang.

Die Steine am Shizhang-Pavillon stammten aus dem Taihu-See.

◄ A snow scene at the Long Corridor.

Admirer la neige dans la Longue Galerie couverte.

Am Langen Wandelgang bewundert man Schnee.

The Summer Palace houses a large collection of antiques dating from 1700 to 1911. The Pavilion of Pure Magnificence has a regular exhibition displaying precious objects of different dynasties from the collection.

Dans le Palais d'Eté sont collectionnés de nombreux objets historiques de 1700 ans av. J.-C. jusqu'à 1911. Ces objets précieux sont exposés dans le Pavillon Qinghua.

Im Sommerpalast werden zahlreiche Kulturgegenstände aus alten Zeiten von 1700 v. Chr. bis 1911 aufbewahrt. In der Ausstellungshalle für Kuriositäten im Qinghuaxuan-Garten werden wertvolle Kulturgegenstände aus allen Dynastien ausgestellt.

A white jade flat kettle in the shape of a water bird (Qing Dynasty 1644-1911)

Aiguière aplatie en jade blanc en forme de canard de la dynastie des Qing (1644-1911).

Ein weißer Nephritkrug in geschnitzter Wildentenform (Qing-Zeit 1644-1911)

A blue-glazed vase with white dragon pattern (Yuan Dynasty 1279-1368)

Vase à motif de dragon blanc à glaçure bleue de la dynastie des Yuan (1279-1368).

Eine Winterblumenvase mit dem weißen Drachenmuster, blau glasiert (Yuan-Zeit 1279-1368)

A bronze bird-shaped wine vessel inlaid with gold (Warring States Period 475 -221 B.C.)

Récipient à vin en forme d'oiseau en bronze incrusté d'or remontant à l'époque des Royaumes combattants (475-221 av. J.-C.).

Das bronzene Vogelweingefäß (Zun) mit Goldeinlage (Periode der Streitenden Reiche 475-221 v. Chr.)

A wine vessel shaped like a sheep (Han Dynasty 206-220 B.C.)

Récipient à vin en forme de mouton de la dynastie des Han (206 av. J.-C.-220).

Das Schafweingefäß (Zun) (Han-Zeit 206 v. Chr. -220)

Clay figurines (Qing Dynasty 1644-1911)

Figurines d'argile peintes de la dynastie des Qing.

Eine Lehmskulptur (Qing-Zeit 1644-1911)

A white jade screen with Happiness, Fortune and Longevity motifs (Qing Dynasty 1644-1911)

Écran de jade blanc sculpté portant trois caractères chinois: bonheur, fortune et longévité, et datant de la dynastie des Qing.

Der Tuschschirm mit weißer Jadeschnitzerei von Schriftzeichen Glück, hohem Gehalt und Langlebigkeit (Qing-Zeit 1644-1911)

A bronze plate with an 18 fish pattern (Western Zhou Dynasty 1066-771 B.C.)

Plat aux dix-huit poissons de la dynastie des Zhou de l'Ouest (1066-771 av. J.-C.).

Der Teller mit dem 18-Fische-Muster (Westliche Zhou-Zeit 1066-771 v. Chr.)

The first car in China

L'automobile chinoise au XIXe siècle.

Ein Auto aus dem 19. Jahrhundert in China

Jade screen (Qing Dynasty 1644-1911)

Paravent de jade de la dynastie des Qing.

Ein Jadewandschirm (Qing-Zeit 1644-1911)

A three-faced beast wine vessel
(Shang Dynasty 1700-1100 B.C.)

Récipient à vin sculpté de trois
animaux de la dynastie des Shang
(1700-1100 av. J.-C.).

Ein Weingefäß mit drei Tiergesichten
(Shang-Zeit 1700-1100 v. Chr.)

Hall of Listening to Orioles is the place where Dowager Cixi ate her meals. It also indicates that the imperial music is as beautiful as the singing of orioles. Now the hall is a restaurant featuring authentic court cuisine. It has catered for more than one hundred heads of States and thousands of tourists from all over the world.

La Salle pour écouter les loriots (Tingli Guan) où l'impératrice douairière Cixi donnait des banquets et écoutait de la musique. Elle est maintenant devenue un restaurant de spécialités de la Cour impériale. Une centaine de chefs d'État étrangers s'y sont déjà rendus.

Die Halle zum Hören des Goldamselrufs (Tingliguan) war der Bankettsaal der Kaiserinwitwe Cixi. Heute ist die Halle ins Restaurant der Touristen umgewandelt, in dem auch über 100 Staatshäupter empfangen wurden.

颐和园

The Marble Boat, also known as Boat of Purity and Ease (meaning purity of rivers and ease of the sea) is a well known piece of architecture on Kunming Lake. The Boat is 36 meters long built of marble which implied the Qing government would be as stable as marble and never swamped by water.

Le Bateau de marbre (Shi Fang), appelé aussi Qingyanfang qui signifie limpidité et calme du lac, est une fameuse construction sur le lac Kunming. Long de 36 m, il fut taillé dans un énorme bloc de marbre, ce qui symbolise que «la dynastie des Qing est solide comme un roc et ne s'effondra jamais».

Das Schiff der Friedlichen Ruhe (Qingyanfang) ist ein bekanntes Bauwerk im Kunming-See. Das 36 m lange Schiff wurde aus einem gigantischen Stein geschnitzt. Das versinnbildlichte, daß die Qing-Dynastie „fest wie Felsen sein und nie untergehen wird".

The ancient shipyard which kept all the boats used by emperors and empresses during the Qing Dynasty.

Le dock de la dynastie des Qing où sont conservés les bateaux de promenade des empereurs et des impératrices.

Ein antike Dock, wo während der Qing-Dynastie die verschiedenen Vergnügungsboote der Kaiser und Kaiserinnen lagen.

颐和园

Kunming Lake in spring Kunming Lake covers an area of 220 hectares. Western Dike, Eastern Dike, the six bridges on the Western Dike, South Lake Island, and 17-Arch Bridge combine to create a magnificent waterway, known as the West Lake of Hangzhou.

Le paysage d'automne du lac Kunming. D'une superficie de 220 ha, le lac Kunming comprend plusieurs sites pittoresques tels que la Digue de l'Ouest, la Digue de l'Est, les six ponts sur la Digue de l'Ouest, l'îlot du lac Sud, le Pont à dix-sept arches. Il est donc surnommé «lac de l'Ouest de Hangzhou».

Der Kunming-See im Herbst Der See hat eine Gewässerfläche von ca. 220 ha. Der West- und Ostdamm, die sechs Brücken auf dem Westdamm, die Nanhu-Insel und die Siebzehn-Bogen-Brücke bilden einen entzückenden Anblick auf dem See, man nennt ihn „Westsee in Hangzhou".

Xing Bridge is northwest of Kunming Lake. Boats can pass under the bridge to Rear Lake.

Le Pont des Plantes flottantes (Xing Qiao), au nord-ouest du lac Kunming. Le bateau passe par ici pour accéder au lac de Derrière.

Die Xing-Brücke liegt im nordwestlichen Teil des Kunming-Sees. Das Boot fährt unter der Brücke hindurch und erreicht so den Hintersee.

Willow Bridge is one of the six bridges on the Western Dike at the west of the lake. Emperor Qianlong paid three visits to the south of China. He was so impressed by the beauty of the West Lake in Hangzhou, that he decreed that the Western Dike of Kunming Lake should be laid out in imitation of it. Besides Willow Bridge, there are Jiehu, Binfeng, Jade Belt, Mirror and Rainbow Bridges.

Le Pont des Saules (Liu Qiao), à l'ouest du lac Kunming, est un des six ponts sur la Digue de l'Ouest. Après ses trois tournées au sud du Yangtsé, l'empereur Qianlong ordonna de construire la Digue de l'Ouest du lac Kunming sur le modèle de la chaussée surélevée de Su Dongpo à Hangzhou. Les cinq autres sont le Pont Jiehu, le Pont Binfeng, le Pont de la Ceinture de jade, le Pont de l'Armoire et le Pont de la Soie blanche.

Die Liu (Weide)-Brücke, eine der sechs Brücken — Jiehu (Grenzensee)-, Binfeng (Binwind)-, Yudai (Jadegürtel)-, Jing (Spiegel)- und Lian (Kette)-Brücke — auf dem Westdamm, der dem Su-Damm des Westsees in Hangzhou nachgebaut wurde.

Jade Belt Bridge is the most famous of the six bridges on the Western Dike. The arch of the bridge is high and thin, and its body is as white as a jade belt.

Le Pont de la Ceinture de jade (Yudai Qiao) est le plus célèbre des six ponts sur la Digue de l'Ouest. D'une voûte élevée et mince, le pont tout blanc semble un ruban de jade.

Die Yudai-Brücke ist die bekannteste von den sechs Brücken. Ihr Bogen ist hoch und dünn. Die weiße Brücke sieht wie ein Jadegürtel aus.

Octagonal Pavilion over Mirror Bridge on the Western Dike ➤

Kiosque octogonal sur le Pont de l'Armoire.

Der achteckige Pavillon der Jing-Brücke auf dem Westdamm

Four sided pavilion over Rainbow
Bridge on the Western Dike

Kiosque quadrangulaire sur le Pont de
la Soie blanche.

Der viereckige Pavillon der Lian-
Brücke auf dem Westdamm

Binfeng Bridge on the Western Dike

Le Pont Binfeng sur la Digue de l'Ouest.

Die Binfeng-Brücke auf dem Westdamm

The Building of Bright Scenery is named from prose
descriptions entitled "Notes of Yueyang Tower" by Fan
Zhongyan of the Song Dynasty: "The tower is harmonious and
bright in spring. Great waves cannot scare it. Boundless blue
water makes the sky and water into one."

Les Pavillons du Spectacle ravissant (Jingming Lou) dont le
nom provient du Récit de voyage au Pavillon de Yueyang, écrit
par Fan Zhongyan de la dynastie des Song. Ce site sur la
Digue de l'Ouest est un paysage poétique.

Der Jingming-Turm, der Name stammt aus dem Prosa
„Aufzeichnung über den Yueyang-Turm" von Fan Zhongyan,
einem bekannten Staatsmann und Schriftsteller der Song-
Dynastie: „Im Frühling ist es warm, die Landschaft leuchtet und
bezaubert, alles steht in Ruhe und Frieden, Wasser und
Himmel sind von derselben Farbe; zehntausend ha großer See
ist blau." Im Turm herrscht eine poetische und malerische
Stimmung.

Hall of Holding Emptiness is the main building on South Lake Island, one of the three islands on Kunming Lake. Dowager Cixi once watched naval exercises here.

Le Pavillon Hanxu est l'édifice principal sur l'îlot du lac Sud, un des trois îlots du lac Kunming, où l'impératrice douairière Cixi assistait aux manœuvres militaires de la marine.

Die Halle der Bescheidenheit (Hanxutang) auf der Nanhu-Insel, eine der drei Inseln im Kunming-See, sah sich die Kaiserinwitwe Cixi hier ein Manöver der Flotte an.

Kunming Lake was formerly called West Sea, so Dragon Temple was built on South Lake Island and the Dragon King of the West Sea is enshrined here to prevent the area from flooding.

Le lac Kunming, autrefois appelé Mer de l'Ouest. Sur l'îlot du lac Sud fut construit le Temple du Roi Dragon dans lequel s'érige la statue du roi Dragon pour protéger le lac Kunming.

Der Kunming-See hieß ursprünglich Westmeer. Zur Verhütung der Überschwemmung wurde ein Tempel des Drachenkönigs auf der Nanhu-Insel gebaut, wo dem Drachenkönig des Westmeeres Opfer dargebracht wurden.

The 150-meter long 17-Arch Bridge is the longest bridge in the Summer Palace. It connects South Lake Island to the shore and is like a long dragon.

Le Pont à dix-sept arches (Shiqikong Qiao), long de 150 m, est le plus long pont de pierre du Palais d'Eté et comme un dragon enjambant la Digue de l'Est et l'îlot du lac Sud.

Die 150 m lange Siebzehn-Bogen-Brücke ist die größte Steinbrücke in Yiheyuan und sieht wie ein langer Regenbogen aus, der zwischen dem Ostdamm und der Nanhu-Insel geschlagen wird.

颐和园

Bronze Ox, cast in 1755, is true to life. On the back of the ox is an inscription with 80 characters written by Emperor Qianlong. The inscription relates how an iron ox can calm a flood.

Le Bœuf en bronze fut fabriqué en 1755. Sur son dos, on lit une inscription de 80 caractères de style sigillaire, sur la garde du lac par le bœuf, écrite par l'empereur Qianlong.

Der Bronzene Büffel wurde 1755 gegossen. Auf seinem Rücken wurden die Inschriften mit 80 Schriftzeichen, die von Kaiser Qianlong eigenhändig geschrieben wurden, eingraviert, nach denen der Büffel Wasserdämonen im Banne halten könnte.

Eight-Facet Pavilion is at the
eastern end of the 17-Arch
Bridge. It covers an area of
over 130 square meters and is
the largest pavilion in the
history of Chinese architecture.

Le Kiosque comme galerie
(Langru Ting) couvrant un
terrain de 130 m² à l'extrémité
est du Pont à dix-sept arches
est le plus grand des kiosques
de Chine.

Langru-Pavillon befindet sich
am Ostkopf der Siebzehn-
Bogen-Brücke, hat eine
Baufläche von mehr als 130
qm und ist der größte seiner
Art in China.

颐和园

Mirror Bridge of the Western
Dike at dusk.

Le Pont de l'Armoire sur la
Digue de l'Ouest, au
crépuscule.

Die Jing-Brücke auf dem
Westdamm im abendliche
Zwielicht

17-Arch Bridge in spring

Le Pont à dix-sept arches au printemps.

Die Siebzehn-Bogen-Brücke im Frühling

Hall at the Riverside is built on the side of Little Suzhou River, at the western end of Kunming Lake. It is a quiet place to meditate.

La Salle au bord de la rivière (Linhe Dian), située à l'ouest du lac Kunming, au bord de la petite rivière Suzhou, est un endroit tranquille idéal pour cultiver un esprit équilibré.

Die Linhe-Halle wurde am westlichen Ende des Kunming-Sees und am Kleinen Suzhou-Fluß angelegt und ist eine stille und ideale Stätte, in der man sich moralisch und charakterisch vervollkommnet.

Tower of Resting Clouds is one of the six city gate towers in the Summer Palace, and is at the western side of Longevity Hill.

Les avant-toits de la tour dans les nuages, qui surmonte une porte, l'une des six portes du Palais d'Eté, à l'ouest de la Colline de la Longévité.

Suyunyan, eines der sechs Türmer über dem Stadttor im Sommerpalast, liegt am Westhang des Wanshou-Bergs.

颐和园

Jade Belt Bridge of
Western Dike in
autumn.

Paysage automnale du
Pont de la Ceinture de
Jade.

Die Yudai-Brücke im
Herbst

Kunming Lake at sunset
Coucher du soleil au lac Kunming.
Sonnenuntergang am Kunming-See

颐和园

A tower surrounded by trees and lake

Pavillon pour contempler les monts et
les lacs.

Ein Pavillon auf dem Berg

◀ Western Dike at sunset

Soleil couchant sur la
Digue de l'Ouest.

Sonnenuntergang am
Westdamm

Rear Hill and Rear Lake of the Summer Palace. The waterway of Rear Lake zigzags along the curves of Rear Hill and there are willow trees on both sides. Flowers bloom all over the hill.

Des deux côtés du lac de Derrière, long et en zigzag, les saules pleureurs offrent leur ombre et les fleurs s'épanouissent.

Der Houshan-See (Hintersee) im Sommerpalast Die stille und lange Wasserstraße schängt sich, am Ufer machen die Trauerweiden Schatten und die Blumen sind in voller Blüte.

Boating on Rear Lake

Promenade en bateau sur le lac de Derrière.

Im Hintersee rudern

颐和园

A night scene of
Suzhou Street

Vue nocturne de la rue
de Suzhou.

Die Suzhou-Straße bei
Nacht

Suzhou Street was a commercial street built for emperors, empresses and concubines of the Qing Dynasty to go shopping. It is 300 meters long and covers a construction area of 3,000 square meters. The water is the street and the banks are markets. The street had more than 60 stores. One hundred years have gone by, but it retains the original look of an 18th century Chinese commercial thoroughfare.

La rue de Suzhou, longue de 300 m, au bord du lac de Derrière, comptait plus de 60 boutiques d'une superficie totale de 3 000 m², où les empereurs, impératrices et concubines de la dynastie des Qing faisaient des achats en se promenant. Depuis une centaine d'années, l'aspect original de cette rue commerçante se maintient toujours.

Die Suzhou-Straße war eine Geschäftsstraße, die speziell dem Kaiser, der Kaiserin und den kaiserlichen Konkubinen zum Einkauf oder Marktbummeln zur Verfügung stand. Sie ist 300 m lang und hat eine Baufläche von ca. 3000 qm. Der Handelsmarkt liegt am Ufer des Sees und hat über 60 Ladenräume. Es sind hundert Jahre verstrichen, bleibt sie nach wie vor in ihrer ursprünglichen Ansicht der Handelskultur des 18. Jahrhunderts erhalten.

Stores are open on
both sides of the street

Les boutiques dans la
rue de Suzhou.

Die Läden an beiden
Ufern betreiben
Geschäfte.

颐和园

Hall of Lasting Longevity is an independent yard which was used by imperial doctors. Mao Zedong, the founder of modern China, lived here in March 1949 and wrote a famous poem: "Don't say that the water of Kunming Lake is shallow. It's better to watch fish here than in Fuchun River."

La Salle de la Garantie de la Longévité (Yishou Tang) où logeait le médecin de l'empereur. En mars 1949, Mao Zedong, fondateur de la République populaire de Chine, y séjourna une brève période et composa un poème: «Ne dites pas que le lac Kunming n'est pas profond, cet endroit est mieux pour contempler les poissons que le fleuve Fuchun.»

Die Halle der Verlängerung des Lebens (Yishoutang) war ursprünglich ein Hof für die kaiserlichen Ärzte. Im März 1949 wohnte Vorsitzender Mao Zedong, Gründer der Volksrepublik China, hier. Damals schrieb er hier ein Gedicht: „Sagt nicht, im Kunming-See zu niedrig das Wasser / Sind doch die Fische besser zu sehen als im Fuchun."

◄ Ziqidonglai city gate is a four-sided, double layer gate tower. It is one of the six city gate towers in the Summer Palace. It is at the eastern end of Longevity Hill, so it is the first tower to greet the rising sun.

La porte surmontée d'une tour quadrangulaire saluant le soleil levant, à deux étages, l'une des six portes du Palais d'Eté, située à l'extrémité de la Colline de la Longévité.

Der Ziqidonglai-Turm, einer der sechs Türmer über dem Stadttor im Sommerpalast, ist ein viereckiges und zweistöckiges Bauwerk. Er liegt am östlichen Fuß des Wanshou-Berges, so ist er der erste Turm, der der Sonne entgegengeht.

Garden of Harmonious Delights is a garden within a garden and was built in imitation of Jichang Garden in Wuxi, South China. It is composed of five halls, seven pavilions, and a hundred winding corridors. Everything here from pavilions, terraces, towers and bridges to lotus, bamboo and rocks reflect the beautiful scenery of South China and bring delight to the surprised visitor.

Le Jardin de l'Harmonie (Xiequ Yuan), appelé «jardin des jardins», fut construit sur le modèle du jardin de l'Allégresse de Wuxi. Il se compose de cinq pavillons et salles et de sept kiosques et pavillons d'eau reliés par la Longue Galerie couverte. Les pavillons, belvédères, kiosques, pavillons d'eau, ponts, étangs, lotus, bambous et rochers forment harmonieusement un paysage pittoresque tout comme celui du sud du pays.

Der Garten der Geselligkeit (Xiequyuan) Der Garten wurde nach dem Muster des Gartens der Ergötzung in der Stadt Wuxi, südlich von Jangtse, angelegt und ist als „Garten innerhalb des Gartens" bekannt. Rund um einen Lotosteich verteilen sich fünf Hallen, sieben Wasserlauben, ein gewundener Korridor und fünf kleine Brücke. Das Bauwerk ist für seine malerische Szenen und den südchinesischen Baustil bekannt.

颐和园

Garden of Harmonious
Delights in winter

Le Jardin de l'Harmonie
couverte de neiges.

Xiequyuan mitten im Winter

頤和園

Garden of Harmonious
Delights in early spring

Le Jardin de l'Harmonie au
printemps.

Xiequyuan am Anfang des
Frühlings

Garden of Harmonious
Delights in autumn

Le Jardin de
l'Harmonie en
automne.

Xiequyuan im Herbst

Knowing Fish Bridge is named after a story about the ancient Chinese philosopher Zhuang Zi watching fish. Visitors can stop on the bridge and enjoy watching fish playing around and looking for food, and at the same time reflect on how happy and free they are in nature.

Le Pont de la Contemplation des poissons (Zhiyu Qiao) dont le nom est dû à un article intitulé «La contemplation des poissons» de Lao Zi, célèbre philosophe de la Chine antique. On peut contempler sur le pont des poissons qui nagent et cherchent leur nourriture dans l'étang de lotus.

Zhiyu-Brücke   Der Name ist dem Artikel „Fischbeobachtung" von Zhuangzi, einem bekannten chinesischen Philosophen in den alten Zeiten, entnommen. Touristen stehen auf der Brücke und bewundern, wie frei die Fische im Lotosteich spielen und Futter suchen.

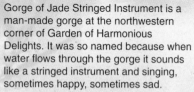

Gorge of Jade Stringed Instrument is a man-made gorge at the northwestern corner of Garden of Harmonious Delights. It was so named because when water flows through the gorge it sounds like a stringed instrument and singing, sometimes happy, sometimes sad.

La Gorge du Luth de Jade (Yuqin Xia), artificielle, se trouve au nord-ouest du Jardin de l'Harmonie. Les eaux du lac coulant par ici rendent un son mélodieux tout comme celui du luth.

Die Jadezither-Schlucht (Yuqin-Schlucht), die von Hand gemeißelt wurde, liegt an der nordwestlichen Ecke des Xiequyuan. Das Wasser fließt durch diese Schlucht und klingt dabei wie ein Zitherspiel. Deshalb erhielt sie ihren Namen.

Hall of Magnanimity is the main building in the Garden of Harmonious Delights. Dowager Cixi used to stop here and take a rest when visiting the garden.

La Salle de la Magnanimité (Hanyuan Tang), l'édifice principal du Jardin de l'Harmonie, où se reposait l'impératrice douairière Cixi lors de sa promenade.

Die Halle der Weitsichtigkeit (Hanyuantang), das Hauptbauwerk in Xiequyuan, war eine Stätte, wo Kaiserinwitwe während des Besuchs in Xiequyuan gewöhnlich für eine Weile verweilte.

颐和园

A view of Kunming Lake
Panorama du lac Kunming.
Panorama vom Kunming-See

The Bridge of
Embroidering Ripples
which used to be the
gateway for boats going to
and fro between the
Summer Palace and the
Forbidden City.

Le Pont de la Soie brodée
(Xiuyi Qiao) fut un passage
nécessaire des bateaux
impériaux qui allaient et
venaient entre le Palais
d'Eté et la Cité interdite.

Xiuyi-Brücke   Das
kaiserliche Schiff fuhr unter
dieser Brücke in die
Verbotene Stadt
hineindurch.

Taihe Double-Deck Pleasure
Boat on Kunming Lake

Le «Taihe», grand bateau de
promenade peint à deux
étages.

Das zweistöckiges
Vergnügungsboot „Taihe" auf
dem Kunming-See

Ancient pine forest at the foot
of Longevity Hill

La forêt de vieux pins au pied
de la Colline de la Longévité.

Der alte Kieferwald am Fuß
des Wanshou-Bergs

颐和园

Wenchang Pavilion in the mist

Le Pavillon Wenchang dans le
brouillard matinal.

Die Halle der Blühenden Kultur
(Wenchangge) im Morgendunst

Knowing Spring Pavilion is surrounded by the lake. Willow trees and peach trees grow at the sides of the pavilion. When spring comes willow trees are the earliest to turn green and peach flowers are the first to bloom, so people named the pavilion Knowing Spring Pavilion.

Le Kiosque du Réveil du Printemps (Zhichun Ting) entouré par les eaux, où les saules pleureurs verdoient et les fleurs s'épanouissent dès l'arrivée du printemps.

Der Pavillon der Frühlingsahnung (Zhichunting)　Der Pavillon liegt am Ostdamm des Kunming-Sees. Vom Wasser umgeben, ruht er inmitten von Felsgesteinen , Pfirsichbäumen und Trauerweiden. Jedes Jahr beginnt der vereiste See zuerst hier zu vermelzen und kundigt so die Ankunft des Frühlings an. Daher der Name.

A snow scene at
Longevity Hill

La Colline de la
Longévité sous la
neige.

Der Wanshou-Berg in
Winterpracht

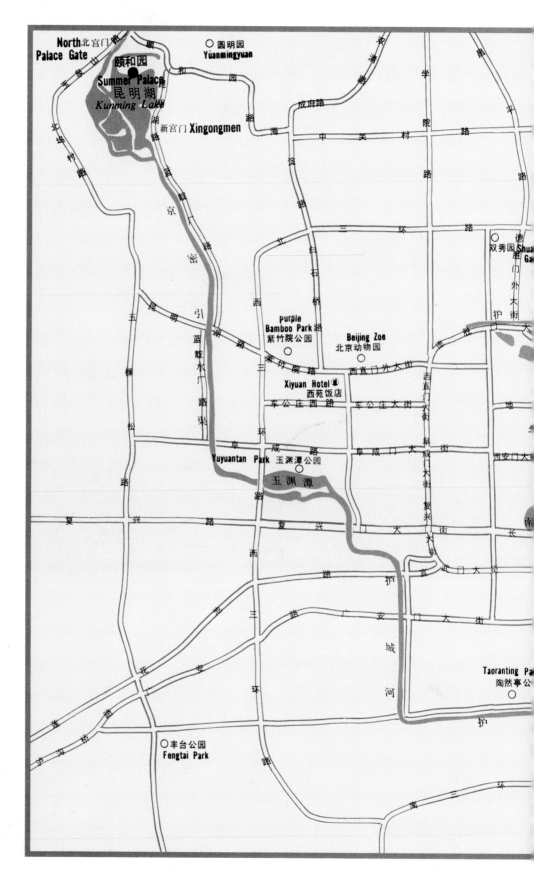

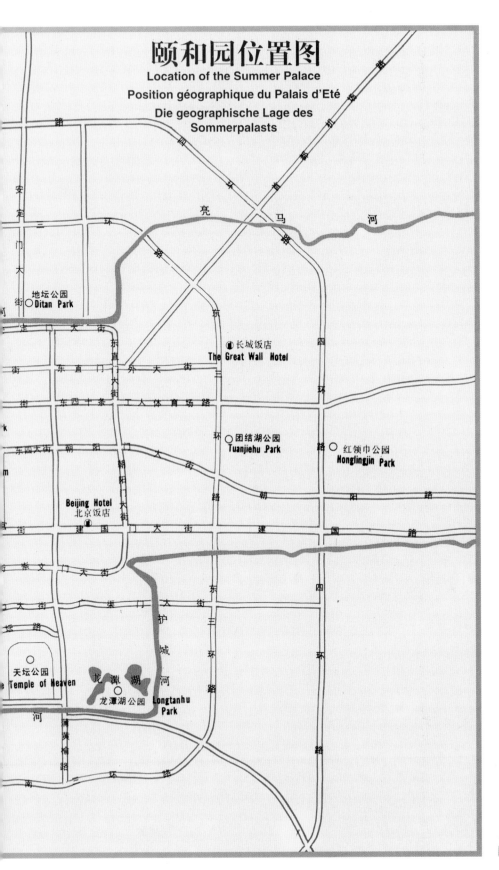

颐和园位置图

Location of the Summer Palace

Position géographique du Palais d'Eté

Die geographische Lage des Sommerpalasts

地坛公园
○ Ditan Park

长城饭店
The Great Wall Hotel

团结湖公园
Tuanjiehu Park

红领巾公园
Honglingjin Park

Beijing Hotel
北京饭店

天坛公园
The Temple of Heaven

龙潭湖
龙潭湖公园 Longtanhu
Park

颐和园

Map of Western Suburbs of Beijing drawn in the Qing Dynasty
Carte des sites célèbres dans l'ouest de Beijing sous la dynastie des Qing
Karte für die Sehenswürdigkeiten im Westvorort Beijings, die in der Qing-Zeit gezeichnet wurde.

图书在版编目（CIP）数据

颐和园：英、法、德文对照／吴显林等主编
北京：新世界出版社，2000.8
ISBN 7-80005-319-9

I. 颐... II. 吴... III. 颐和园－图集－英、法、德
IV. K928.73

中国版本图书馆CIP数据核字（2000）第41856号

颐 和 园

名誉主编／李福瀛 段应合
主　　编／吴显林 张大明
编　　审／舒　君
翻　　译／李淑娟（英）吕志祥（法）李道斌（德）
摄　　影／天　行 李维深 杨福生
美术装帧／徐沪生
封面设计／徐沪生
电脑制作／卢一凡
出版发行／新世界出版社
社　　址／北京百万庄路24号 邮政编码／100037
电子邮件／nwpcn@public.bta.net.cn
印　　刷／北京利丰雅高长城印刷有限公司
开　　本／16开
印　　张／8
版　　次／2000年第1版 2000年第1次印刷
书　　号／ISBN 7-80005-319-9
　　　　　　05000

Honorary Chief Editors: Li Fuying   Duan Yinghe

Chief Editors: Wu Xianlin   Zhang Daming

Executive Editor: Shu Jun

Translators: Li Shujuan   Lu Zhixiang   Li Daobin

Designer: Xu Husheng

Photos: Tian Xing   Li Weishen   Yang Fusheng

ISBN 7-80005-319-9/J · 077

Published by

NEW WORLD PRESS

24 Baiwanzhuang Road, Beijing 100037, China

First Edition: 2000

Printed in the People's Republic of China